Personality Disorders

Narcissistic Personality Disorder

How To Survive A Narcissistic Relationship

By James Seals

2nd Edition

Contents

Introduction

A pathological narcissist is a person who suffers from a personality disorder, one of the characteristics of which is antisocial tendencies. They have no empathy with other people; indeed, they will go out of their way to remove the limelight from others on to themselves. A person who suffers from narcissistic personality disorder is very self-aware, very demanding and have a real belief that the entire world revolves around them. They are highly manipulative and believe that others exist purely for their entertainment.

Narcissism is evident everywhere. If you don't know what signs to look out for, you may well be working with one, live next door to one or even have one within your own family. Dealing with a narcissist is hard work because, at first glance, you would believe them to be the kindest people that walk the earth. This is what they want you to think, how they draw you into their web and under their control.

If you want to know how to deal with a narcissist, this book is for you. Between the pages, you will discover what narcissistic personality disorder is, how it is diagnosed and treated. You will also discover how to spot a narcissist and how to deal with them, how to talk to them and how to leave them.

Dealing with a person who suffers from narcissistic personality disorder will be difficult but this book aims to give you a heads up and a foothold in your journey.

Chapter 1: What Is Narcissism?

Narcissism is a word or term that we use to describe a self-centered focus, a self-admiration that is extreme. The word itself is derived from Greek Mythology, a myth in which Narcissus, a handsome man, sees his own reflection in a pool and falls in love with it. Narcissistic personality disorder is just one condition in a group known as "Cluster B" conditions. These are dramatic personality disorders and people who suffer from them tend to display very intense and unstable emotions and a distorted image of themselves.

A further characteristic of Narcissistic personality disorder is a highly abnormal love of one's self, an exaggerated sense of self-importance and superiority over others along with a real preoccupation of being wealthy and successful. Some see it as self-confidence but none of these traits are a true indicator of confidence instead being used as a mask to cover up a deep sense of insecurity and a sense of self-esteem that is fragile. Along with that, a narcissist will display no empathy for others.

Signs and Symptoms of Narcissistic Personality Disorder

In most cases of narcissistic personality disorder, a person will display most, if not all, of the following symptoms:

- Self-centered
- Boastful
- Constant attention seeking
- High opinion of themselves
- Exaggerate their achievements and their talents
- Belief that they deserve to be given special treatment
- Hurt easily but rarely show it
- Have a set of unrealistic long-term goals
- Will use others to achieve their goals
- Have a preoccupations with power, success, beauty, love and intelligence
- Believe that they are unique and can only be understood by a special person
- Expect that other people will go along with their plans
- Cannot recognize the feelings of others nor will they listen to another viewpoint
- Envious of what others have and believe that others are envious of them
- Hypersensitive to both real and imagined criticism, threats and defeat, may react with shame, rage or humiliation
- Arrogant

Some more symptoms explained in detail are:

React aggressively to criticism

All narcissists hunt for praise and attention, when they are trying to get people to pay attention to them they make up a multitude of lies, fake stories and incidents that make them look good. Whenever you ask them a question that may reveal their lies; they will react aggressively to your criticism to protect themselves. In reality, narcissists are very insecure and any sort of criticism annoys them because they feel attacked and vulnerable. Most narcissists have an image of themselves in their head, this is not their true self but what they imagine themselves to be. They act like this fake self all the time so that they can get praise and attention, because they believe that this fake self is better than their real self. They also react negatively to criticism, it reminds them that what they portray to the world isn't actually them and someone did notice that.

Have low self-esteem

It may seem like most narcissists think highly of themselves and have high self-esteem, but that's not true at all. Narcissists are power hungry people who have inflated egos, but under this mask, which they wear for the world, there are feelings of fear and repression. They feel that they are not actually as successful as they think they are. This is why they try to hunt for praise and attention; they want the world to see that they're actually worth all the attention so that this inner low self-esteem can be driven off. They are constantly trying to prove themselves to people; they doubt themselves and their achievements. They are also very envious of others, if anyone else ever achieves more than them, they react in a very negative manner due to their low self-esteem. They're extremely skilled at wearing a mask and portraying to the world their nice qualities, but in reality beneath that mask, there is a person who is so insecure that they're always fishing and begging for compliments to make themselves believe that they are better than what they think they are.

Low self-esteems can also be a result of childhood failures, never being the best in your class, not having many friends and criticism by parents. This is why narcissists later on try to look for praise in all kinds of places to prove it to their child self that they are after all better than others and worth the attention.

Extremely Defensive

If you have ever encountered a narcissist with a huge ego you must have noticed how quickly they become defensive when criticized or questioned. This is because most of them think that they are self-righteous, that it's their opinion that matters and everyone else is wrong. Narcissists never listen to suggestions; it's always their way which is the right way. It is very difficult to deal with such a person as it can be exhausting when they argue with you to death till they're proven right. Most narcissists depend on these petty arguments or debates to give their ego a boost. They will never admit that it was their mistake and the world 'I am sorry' will never be heard from their mouth.

They have a coping defense mechanism because they have huge egos that are actually extremely fragile and they try to protect their ego by using this defense mechanism. When handling such a narcissist, it's important to not contradict them directly, but in such a way that they're proven wrong while your point gets through to them. If you ever directly contradict a narcissist or his views, it will always result in aggressive behavior. You might actually think that you can win an argument against them, but even if your points were right, there is no way that a narcissist would back up and admit that he or she is wrong. So, it's important to prove the narcissist wrong by not directly contradicting them, but putting just a hint of doubt in their mind that makes them back up.

React with rage or violence

Many narcissists get into fights with others on small matters, even if they are wrong. This is the most common symptom of a narcissist. If you criticize them, question them or give suggestions to them that bring out their insecurities, they will lash out with rage or violence. Most narcissists live a life of lie; they show their fake self to the world and hide their insecurities. Every time someone criticizes them, these emotions come flooding out and the only defense they have against being humiliated is to be violent. Most people would never react in such a way but narcissists always react this way due to their inhibitions. If you contradict them or have a better viewpoint then them, it makes them insecure and envious of you. Violence is their last resort to protect their huge ego bubble from shattering into millions of pieces.

If you're in a relationship with such a person, you might have noticed that you're constantly blamed for everything that is wrong in your relationship, but don't worry about it, it's most probably not your fault as it's the narcissist trying to prove his self-righteousness by blaming you instead of themselves. Narcissists have a coping mechanism when it comes to facing problems; it's to blame others for their problems and not themselves. The only way to survive such a relationship is to understand that it's never your fault and this is a blame game that will keep on going.

Criticize others

Narcissists project their negativity and bad qualities onto others; this is their coping mechanism. If they're criticized or feel insecure, the only way left for them is to blame others. They try to steer the conversation away from themselves by pointing out others' flaws, this is a very cheap technique used by them to make sure their insecurities and everyone doesn't see flaws.

If you talk about their weaknesses or flaws, the only ways left out for them is to similarly talk about your flaws so that the attention is drawn from their negativity to yours. Narcissists cannot deal with negative attention, they only like attention that puts them in a comfortable position but if it brings out their repressed doubts and emotions, they cannot handle it.

Don't know the concept of personal boundaries

Narcissists do not respect others right to privacy, all they care about is achieving their goals, and they use other people's feelings as supplies for their own ego. Narcissist are extremely social and dominate in conversation; they talk about things that others may be too embarrassed to tell. They do not have any idea what these boundaries are and may even talk about things that are gross to others. They do not hesitate to talk about intimate connections and may even use demeaning things to boast about their achievements. They don't realize that it makes other people feel uncomfortable but use these conversations as a way to gain attention.

Chapter 2: Narcissistic Personality Disorder – Causes, Diagnosis and Treatment

Causes

There has been a lot of research into what causes narcissistic personality disorder but researchers are still unable to answer the question. There are theories though and many professionals believe that the causes are most likely to be a combination of genetic, social and biological factors. This includes looking at how a person with narcissistic personality disorder interacted with other people, like friends and family, in their early years. They also include psychological factors such as what sort of personality the individual has, what their temperament is like and how they cope with stress.

The suggestion is that narcissistic personality disorder cannot be put down to one single factor, rather it is a highly complex and entwined combination of factors and, research does show that, where a person suffers from narcissistic personality disorder, their children have a higher risk than normal of having it as well.

Diagnosis

A diagnosis for any personality disorder must be made by a

professional trained in mental health. This usually means that a psychiatrist or psychologist must make the diagnosis, not the family GP. General practitioners are not trained in mental health procedures and, while it is possible to consult one initially, they should then refer the individual to a properly trained professional.

Professional diagnoses are not made using blood tests, lab test or any kind of genetic test. Most people who have narcissistic personality disorder will not actively seek out treatment because they do not believe there is anything wrong with them. They would rather believe everyone else around them needs to seek treatment before they do. In general, most people with any personality disorder will not seek any kind of help until the disorder interferes with their lives in a way that it can no longer be ignored. This usually happens when coping skills are stretched to the point of snapping and the individual can no longer deal with stress or any other event in their lives.

A professional will make a diagnosis of narcissistic personality disorder by looking at your symptoms and your life history and comparing them to those listed above. They will determine if any or all of your symptoms match those that are required for a diagnosis of narcissistic personality disorder.

Treatment

Treatment involves psychotherapy and is a long-term treatment plan. It must be done by a suitably qualified and experienced therapist and, in conjunction with a doctor; they may also prescribe medication to help with specific symptoms. Treatment plans are specific to the individual and, as such, we cannot give you an overview, as it wouldn't be accurate enough.

Chapter 3: How To Negotiate With A Narcissist

Narcissists are very difficult to cooperate with; they can be frustrating as well as annoying at times. They like to draw the attention towards themselves and only focus on the internal and never on the external. If you want to negotiate with a narcissist so that you can control their behavior and even understand them there are a few tricks that can come helpful.

Focusing on the long-term

If you want to deal with a narcissist on a long-term basis then there are many useful tips that you can use. Most people like to deal with a narcissist on a long-term basis because it prevents them from being too emotionally invested with the narcissist. If you're such a person then here are some useful tips are:

Identifying a narcissist

The word narcissist gets dropped around everywhere these days even though many people don't understand its true meaning. A narcissist isn't just someone who is vain and only talks about themselves; narcissism is a very complex mental disorder that includes emotional instability, insecurity, jealousy, etc. Therefore, before using this word and diagnosing someone with narcissism you need to understand whom a narcissist is.

Narcissists cannot show empathy or love towards others. This is the biggest give away for a narcissistic personality. They simply can't care about others; they are so self-obsessed that they will always be envious of others achievements. This is the major problem with narcissists; they don't see other people as humans who may have better opinions than them. It's always their opinion that rules, which is why they always have an urge to be right. For example, if a friend of a narcissist gets a huge promotion at work, the narcissist will never actually compliment or congratulate them. They will try to turn the spotlight on themselves by taking about their own achievements. Many people get annoyed by this kind of behavior and believe it to be rude but that's just how a narcissist functions.

Narcissists never judge their own actions; they never doubt themselves and always believe that their opinion is better than others. This is what leads to their hunt for praise and attention; they want other people to believe that their actions are always correct because it inflates their ego.

Ask yourself whether the person you're trying to diagnose depicts such emotions. Do they think that the world revolves around them, only talk about themselves, don't care about others feelings, constantly beg for praise and attention, love to be in the spotlight and sometimes behave aggressively when contradicted? If they clearly show the above symptoms then you are dealing with a narcissist.

Do you need the narcissist in your life?

Narcissists generally are of two types, they either behave emotionally unstable or completely in control of themselves. If you are going through some tough times, then you may want to break off the connection with the narcissist because most of them will use you for their own needs. But if the narcissist is a very vibrant person they may be good company to cheer you up. Remember to observe the narcissist carefully, because it takes minutes for narcissist to change their personality. If you're extremely depressed or sad, absolutely stay away from them. Narcissists try to emotionally manipulate you into thinking that you are the one at fault, so they might just make your situation worse.

If you think that someone is emotionally manipulating you, then break the connection with him or her because it is definitely not worth it. They will take up most of your time in their hunt for attention and reciprocate their insecurities and negative traits towards you. At times, the narcissist who is causing you so many problems might just be your friend or even your parent. Think of ways to stay away from them till you get better.

Narcissists can cause emotional exhaustion as well as frustration. They need attention, praise and will nag you for your time. If you feel like their needy nature is bad for your health, it's time to break off the relationship you have with them. Narcissist can go as far as to emotionally manipulate you, this is even worse for your health. Get away from them as fast as possible because narcissists can destroy your life by filling it with doubts and discord.

Accept them if need be

If the narcissist is someone very close to you and you can't break your relationship with him or her, then you have to learn to accept them the way they are. You can try to help them and learn better ways to control yourself, but they will always be a self-centered narcissist. You will never receive any love from them; they will never show you any empathy no matter how hard you try. It is better that you learn to deal with their problems instead of trying to change them. It will just exhaust you and make your relationship worse that it already is.

For example, if your mother is a narcissist and you have been trying to tell her about your problems but she just switches back to a topic that puts her in the spotlight you have to accept that your mother will never show you empathy and you should look for empathy in places where you can actually get them. This way you are not wasting your time and it does not deteriorate you emotionally.

Be strong

Even though you may need a narcissist for support and assuring you about things, never approach them on such matters. They'll just use this as an opportunity to depict their own self-worth and will leave you in a worse situation. You have to understand that self-worth comes from within, if you have low self-esteem then don't look for help, don't ask others to praise you or pay attention to you, this can lead to many problems in the future. A narcissist will never be able to provide you with assurance; you just have to raise yourself in your own eyes.

Do not share secrets with narcissists; they will never fully understand the weight of what you have told them. Even if you confide in them, they will never actually empathize with you. They may even use this knowledge to manipulate you for personal gain. Narcissists will always put their problems before yours. No matter how small their problems are, they will always ask for your help to solve them but when it's their turn to help you out, they'll always back out. This will just make you feel disappointed in your choices, so make sure that you never ask a narcissist for help in the first place.

Help the narcissist, too

The narcissist is not an evil person but it's just their mentality that makes them a person who doesn't love others. Most narcissists depict a very brave and confident version of them before others but that's not their true picture. Many narcissists just put on a mask to pretend that they have a high self-esteem while in reality they are extremely insecure; under this mask they hide repressed emotions related to sadness and low self-esteem. This is why they require others to praise them; they take it as an approval of their fake self.

This does not imply that narcissists are not human at all; they have just been turned into such a person who does not like to hear about others and only care about their own needs. You don't have to let them do whatever they want, control them and help them out. Their low self-esteem should not be an excuse for hurting others; if they do such a thing then you should tell them otherwise.

Narcissists don't have a concept of love either; they cannot comprehend why others would do something without getting anything in return. Their line of thought always concerns themselves, and how best they can fulfill their needs. This is why they use other people as sources to boost their ego, because they don't understand that this might hurt the other person.

If you remember that narcissists are humans too and just like anyone else, have good and bad qualities it will help you to deal with them better. They loathe their true nature and put up a fake self so they don't have to deal with their own negativity, help them remove this mask by reaching out to them personally.

Focusing on the short-term

It may just happen that you are fed up with a narcissist and are on the verge of breaking up your relationship with them, but during these times you may even want to help them by negotiating with them. These tips will with help you negotiate with a narcissist in a better way and change the person in a short span of time.

Don't play games with them

Many narcissists assert control on others by playing mind games with them. They try to manipulate you so that you always have to be on the defensive side with them, every little thing you say can slowly turn into a huge argument. They are also very aggressive and repressive, they will try to put you down and never hear your opinion. They'll create such a situation in front of you that you start blaming yourself for things that you never really did. You need to have an upper hand in such a situation, control them and don't let yourself be controlled. Stop listening to whatever they are saying and break off all connections with them before their negativity starts reflecting on your emotional health.

The most important trick that a narcissist uses is the blame game; stop them from controlling you and stop arguing with them. A narcissist will never accept the blame even if it's their own fault, they will always try to put the blame on others. You have to be careful and not let them get you into the 'blame game'. Understand that a narcissist will never accept defeat, so no matter what proof you have they will always try to put the blame on you. Don't argue with them and do not accept the blame, instead set boundaries with them. Break of all ties with them to make sure that your message gets through, that is, if they keep blaming you for things that you never did then you won't ever talk to them again. Keep a close eye on them; they might even use people close to you to make you believe that it was all your fault.

Narcissists are pathological liars; they will twist and turn everything so that it reflects well on them. If you're ever caught in such a situation with a narcissist, don't start second guessing yourself. The narcissist will always lie but if you remember something very differently than what they are telling you, stick to your story. It's important to not get into an argument with a narcissist, they will make you believe that they are right and it will only cause more problems for you. Just let it slide and forget about the whole situation. If you do have concrete evidence against them then don't think twice before putting them down, if you feel that even with a proof the situation is getting out of your hand then play it safe and back out of the argument.

Don't try to get on their good side

Narcissists also have a superiority complex; they always think that others are inferior to them. Don't try to please them, if you really like someone but they're a narcissist don't try to impress them, you might just get their favor for a short time but they will never regard you as someone close to them.

You will always fall short of their expectations, no matter how much you try to improve yourself; you will always be one step short of reaching that milestone they have set up for you. Don't listen to their criticism, most of the times they try to put your down so that they can feel better about themselves.

If they refuse to give you space, then you need to get a third person between you, use their help to explain how your emotional health is getting deteriorated because of their company. If even this doesn't work, you have to push them away.

Listen
If you don't want to break the connection with a narcissist, then your only option is to listen to them. Genuinely lend an ear to them from time to time; react positively to what they are saying, but never talk about yourself. This way the narcissist will not feel bad because you are ignoring them and you don't have to get emotionally invested with them. If the narcissist demands your attention at a time you cannot give it, let them known. Your time is more important than theirs. If you feel that the conversation is getting boring, ask them to repeat a previous point that you heard well. This way you can break out from the conversation without the narcissist knowing it.

Be honest when praising them

Be genuine and honest around the narcissist. If you praise them then do it with sincerity, talk about their positive qualities that you actually like. This way you don't have to pretend in front of them and it would remind you why you have this particular person in your life. It's not possible that someone does not possess any positive traits, all of you have to do is look.

For example, if a narcissist is a great singer, tell them that you love their singing; it will make them like you more and less prone to attack you. They'll recognize your honesty and appreciate it as well. Compare them to others; tell that they're way better than someone they hate. This will make them feel better about the quality they have and will give them confidence. It will also make them trust you more because you are now on their good side. You have to be careful as well because sometimes this can lead to obsessive behavior by the narcissist.

If you compliment one particular trait of theirs, they will try to reciprocate   that   trait   in   front   of   you.

Be passive

Sometimes it is better to stay quiet about things than saying them out loud. If you're constantly annoyed and frustrated by the narcissist the only option left is to stop talking to them but at the same time pay attention to them by just smiling and nodding. It might annoy the narcissist but at least you're not getting into an argument with them, being passive will help your relationship as you both will always be in agreement. Most narcissists demand constant attention and you won't be able to provide it at times. Smiling and nodding helps because the narcissist doesn't feel like you are ignoring them.

Chapter 4: 10 Things You Should Know About Dealing with a Narcissist

Some time in your life you have come up against a narcissist; you may even have found yourself in the position of having to confront them. Narcissism is no longer an uncommon disorder – around 6% of Americans display some signs of it. If you have never had to face a narcissist before, you need to know that it can be incredibly difficult and challenging so, to help you out, I want to tell you ten things you need to know:

Narcissists Do Not Tolerate Shame

A narcissist is general very sensitive when it comes to inadequacy, insecurity and feeling shameful that they rarely allow themselves to give in to it. If they are on the receiving end of criticism, disappointment or asks him or her to do something they can't do, they will respond by shutting down and acting distant, or they will go the opposite and start criticizing and display hostility.

The Insecurity Inside a Narcissist Starts in Childhood

It is widely thought now that narcissism is a combination of factors, a mix of nature and nurture. While genetics may play a part, a person's childhood tends to play a much bigger one.

Perhaps, as a child, they missed out on unconditional love, leaving them feeling very uncomfortable with emotions. This leads to them becoming obnoxious or acting as if they are a victim if they are blamed for something going wrong. Or, they may have been over-indulged as a child, taught that they could have anything they wanted, leading to them being spoilt and acting as though are entitled to have everything.

Narcissists Are Often Given Burdensome Expectations as a Child

Perhaps they were expected to perform to a very high level as a child or were expected to look after another member of the family. Because of that, they feel that they, as an adult, have to prove themselves by trying to be the center of attention or by showing off all the time, constantly looking for approval.

Narcissists Have a Strong Desire to be Superior

If a narcissist thinks that you have something they don't have, they may react with strong contempt towards you. There is no middle ground; there is no 'both of you being on the up'. He or she has to be better that all around them, whatever it takes.

Narcissists Have an Exaggerated Grandiose Feeling of Self-Worth

They have to have everything better than you or know people that you don't know, people who are high up in society and they really want you to know about it. They have an inflated view of themselves that rarely has anything to do with reality. They do this to hide the fact that they are empty inside.

Narcissists Have a Sense of Entitlement

This s the core of their behavior; they feel that they deserve everything and show no regard for anyone else. This is their way of masking the disappointment of not getting what they ask for. In an extreme case, they may also display behavior that is exploitative and manipulative.

Narcissists Ignore Boundaries

You may need to enforce boundaries to make sure you are not being taken advantage of. Narcissists can be aggressive and selfish and will not always respect your space. It could be down to you to put your foot down and pull back.

Narcissists Respond to Validation

If you are in a relationship of any kind with a narcissist, you may need to affirm things before you confront them about anything. An example of this would be, instead of asking a narcissist why they never listen to you, first say that you care about them and that, by not listening to you, you feel like nothing.

Narcissists Can Be Motivated to Change If the Consequence Is Meaningful

Think about how much it would affect them if you walked away. You don't have to threaten a narcissist, just point out that their behavior is forcing you to make a decision about your relationship, one that will affect them badly. You are not giving them an aggressive ultimatum; you are calmly telling them what will happen. If the consequence is meaningful enough, it may have some effect.

Narcissists Don't Grow Up Emotionally

Think of the narcissist in your life as being an overgrown toddler. It's all for show, they are trying to provoke you into a reaction because it means they have your attention – and that's what they want. Pick your battles carefully, depending on your tolerance levels.

Chapter 5: Controlling a Narcissist

Narcissists are born charmers and manipulators, so it might be very difficult trying to control a narcissists but it's not an impossible task. Doesn't matter if it's a friend or a partner, if you want to help them control their behavior there are various steps that you can take. The first step is to realize that it's you who is in control now and not the narcissist. Further, you have to use this advantage to your benefit, try to get on the good side of the narcissist. This is the only way that they'll even consider listening to you. Moving on, you can help them by taking to them and showing them the correct way. The most important part of controlling a narcissist it to be in control yourself, if you lose your temper at any time it'll only result in the narcissist withdrawing back.

Being on the good side of the Narcissist

Listen to them

Narcissists love praise and attention, so the first step to gaining their favour is to pay attention to what they are saying. Listen closely to whatever they're trying to say, don't just hear it but reply to them with more praise and positive comments. Be prepared to be their center of attention, they'll be constantly nagging you to listen to them and you will be on the receiving end of the conversation almost always. It is a tough job because it gets boring listening to one person talk about their achievements and what not but if you really want to control them, this is the only solution.

Narcissists can easily know if you're lying to them or just putting up a show to make it look like you're listening, so don't just smile at them but actually listen to what they are saying. Give positive feedback; make them think that you really care about each and every detail of their life. Narcissists also react aggressively if they think that they are being cheated so look at their reactions if you think that they're starting to know that you're faking it, you have to start pretending better.

Sincerely praise them

Narcissists already have a huge ego and they love nothing more than hearing people praise them, so that's your cue to give them genuine praise. Find their best qualities, achievements and anything else you can complement them on. If they ever react negatively to something make sure that you never bring that topic up, it's because they are insecure about that particular topic and will react negatively if forced to talk about it.

The more attention you give to the narcissist, the more chances you have on ending up on their good side. Always talk to them, go over to their house and spend time with them, be needy and clingy and constantly message them. All of these will make them think that you're someone who likes to pay attention to them. When you're praising something about them, make sure that it is in front of others, that's because the more people that hear about their greatness, the more their ego increases.

Narcissists are also obsessive in terms for portraying their best qualities to people. If you genuinely praise too many of their qualities, then these are the qualities that the narcissist will reciprocate for you thinking that you love these qualities. So, make sure that when you offer them praise it's not too much, or it'll be you who is in trouble. Take their best quality that you love and constantly praise them about it such as how charming they are or how sweet they are. This way you get to praise them without being forced to deal with a quality you do not like.

Don't think that you're escalating their personality disorder, most adult narcissist have already reached a point where their ego is at max and cannot be increased further.

Build a personal connection

The only way to talk properly to a narcissist is by using the 'I' language. Most narcissists are extremely defensive and aggressive; if you criticize them then they will probably try to push the blame on you. It's impossible to not have a fight with a narcissist, there will be some sort of disagreement and it will lead to misunderstanding. It is important that you be prepared for such a scenario to make sure that your connection doesn't deteriorate. The only solution to this is to approach them personally and try to build a strong connection with them. There will of course be heated arguments, you won't back down that easily and nor will the narcissist. Now, it's important that you use the correct language with the narcissist or the situation can go out of hand. Paraphrase your words to make sure that you use the 'I' language, make sure that they understand that you're a human too and have feelings. This is a simple technique to generate empathy in the narcissist; it will help you in your argument and also help you later on.

The 'I' language makes sure that you do not say something rash, narcissists are extremely prone to show aggressive behavior but when you approach them personally, they'll be more likely to listen to you. As an example, if you got into an argument with a narcissist and you feel bad about it then say, 'I feel bad that I fought with you' instead of saying 'You made me realize that we shouldn't have fought'. Narcissists don't believe in apologies so when you reach them on a personal level they are more likely to listen to you.

Don't accept blame

Narcissists are very good at the blame game that is, blaming others for all of their mistakes. You need to make sure that you don't easily accept the blame and don't blame the narcissist either. Use a language that depicts your dedication towards not arguing with the narcissist and keeping good relations. Narcissists are extremely fragile and if you blame them for anything, they'll reciprocate the same behavior and blame you. The end result will be that you both will be exhausted since none of you accept that you were wrong and it will turn into a huge fight. As stated before, the first step is to maintain good relations with the narcissist, if you take such a step, it will inevitably lead to a fight that will destroy your relations. So, if you really want to control a narcissist make sure that you do not enter the blame game.

A clear example of perfect behavior in such a situation is to not say 'You're the one who is at fault' but rather say that 'I don't know how this problem occurred and I am not okay to take the blame for it'. It's very important that you pick the correct words when dealing with a narcissist; they listen very carefully and at the first hint of blame with lash out. This example shows the perfect behavior because you did not accept the blame and give control to the narcissist but at the same you maintained good relations by not blaming the narcissist.

For example, suppose you meet a narcissist at work and you both are working on a project, now by mistake some error popped up. The narcissist would obviously try to blame you for the mistake, but you shouldn't reply with 'No, this is not my fault, you are the one to blame' but rather explain to the narcissist that it's not either of your fault that there was an error since you both were responsible for the project. The narcissist will quickly take this option because they are not being blamed and will not feel insecure due to the same.

Changing the Narcissist

Don't directly contradict them

Narcissists don't understand the concept of personal space, even though they may not want to but they can make you feel extremely uncomfortable, you have to make sure that you do not point their negative behavior directly. Narcissists do not appreciate if they're humiliated or told that they are wrong, if you tell a narcissist that you do not appreciate their entering your personal space then they will act rudely towards you. This is because most narcissists are very insecure so when you suggest to them that they possess a very negative quality, they may act aggressively. A simple solution to this is would be highlighting some other positive aspect of the narcissist, you could tell him/her that they have many other beautiful qualities and this one quality of theirs irks you a bit. The narcissist would feel good because of the praise given to them while at the same time understanding that they may possess a negative trait. They may still feel insecure and not talk to you for a few days but over time they will realize that this one negative trait does not define their entire character.

You also need to have control over yourself, and understand that most narcissists don't even understand that there are boundaries and limits with people they should not cross. They love contestant chatting and telling you details about their life that a normal person would be humiliated to reveal to anyone else.

For example, if you work with a narcissist and they always try to nag you for company, do not make them feel needy or clingy, if they think that you're not fine with their company, they'll withdraw and find someone else to talk with. This will only result in a discord between you and the narcissist and might just ruin your relationship. Tell them that although you love their company, at this moment you have extremely important work that you need to do and would love to join them later. This way the narcissist does not feel bad and needy, they will probably agree to this and come back at some later time. Do not repeat this behavior again and again because that will make the narcissist suspicious, even though you might be acting nice towards them, they might start thinking that you're pretending to be a nice person in front of them.

Forcing Solutions

If you want to really control the narcissist, then you need to make sure that you do not let them carry on with their usual disconcerting behavior. Narcissist love to be in control and be the focus of attention, if they are in a group then they prefer to drive the conversation and be the leader of the group. Now, this is a trait that may annoy many people, but you need to be patient with them because this is a quality that can be handled.

If you ever have a solution to a problem that you and the narcissist were facing, then make sure that you only put up the solution in front of the narcissist. This solution should be the one that you want to enforce, this way you will get a little control over the actions of the narcissist. If a narcissist focuses on a problem then they like to come up with their own solution and not one that is forced upon them. You need to make sure that your solution is perfect and does not contradict the narcissist's thinking. If it does contradict the narcissist's thinking, then the narcissist will never accept the solution.

Talk as little as you can about the problem, only talking about the solution. There are many benefits that you can achieve by enforcing your solution on the narcissist. For once, you would be in control and the narcissist may even like that someone else helped them get the solution. So if in the future you suggest something similar the narcissist will easily accept what you have to say.

If you do not have a concrete solution then only tell the narcissist about the possible solutions that you prepared, let them help you choose the correct one but do not let them change the solution in any way.

Don't challenge the Narcissist

Most narcissists try to control others and by this they feel more important, it's necessary that you don't challenge them directly, if you do that then you'll meet with aggressive and compulsive behavior. Narcissist believe that it's only their opinion that matters so when someone else questions their plans or ideas they take a lot of offense, make sure that you don't challenge their authority because it would only lead to a fight.

Psychologists explain this by saying that narcissists are hungry for power and try to be leaders, if someone challenges them they feel vulnerable, their insecurities show easily and they react in a very negative manner.

Therefore, you have to make sure that you don't use words like, 'You're wrong' and 'Your ideas are bad'; this will just make the narcissist argue back with you to no avail. If you really have to challenge a narcissist then do subtlety so that they're not aware of it. Don't try to prove them wrong just tell them how your opinion could be right too, if they feel that they're being proven wrong then will fight back. Make sure that you never contradict them in pubic, because in public all they care about is their image and reputation so they will never back down and listen to your points.

Don't blame the Narcissist

Don't ever play the blame game with the narcissist; they will never let you win. Narcissists have inflated egos that don't allow them to be proven wrong, it doesn't matter if it's clearly their fault they won't ever accept it. They cope with being blamed by blaming others, this is a defense mechanism used by most narcissists. The only solution to this problem is to not talk about the mistake at all, divert their attention by talking about something else. Quickly change the topic before an argument starts. The narcissist will also try to blame you; don't ever accept the blame. If you accept the blame then the narcissist will feel more in control and will hardly listen to you.

Imagine that you work with the narcissist and you both had to make a presentation, now some discrepancy occurred in the presentation due to the narcissist's fault. The narcissist will quickly try to put the blame on you and will not listen to any logical argument, the only option that will be left with you is to either fight back or take the blame. Do not do either of these things; simply point out how it could not be your fault while not implying that it could be the narcissist's fault. After doing this, change the topic and point out how you need to focus on more important things. The narcissist will easily accept this as they're not being blamed and they do not have to argue or fight. Another way to control the narcissist in such a situation is to compliment and praise them. Tell them that you're sure they couldn't have been at fault and maybe it was just a mutual mistake. Compliment them about their intellect and ask for their help in solving the problem.

Help the narcissist understand that they will benefit

The only way to convince a narcissist it to appeal to them in such a way that they think they're in control and will benefit from the situation. Narcissists are very proud and independent; they do not like anyone else telling them what to do, as long as they feel that they're in control they won't fight back. So, be subtle when putting ideas in their mind and make them think that they are in-charge while enforcing your solution. If a narcissist believes that he/she can benefit from a situation they'll easily accept whatever they are being told.

Complimenting the narcissist can go a long way, appeal to their good qualities and tell them how you want them to help you enforce that particular situation. For example, if a narcissist takes pride in being clever, then appeal to that nature of the narcissist, tell them how this particular solution is very clear and many other clever people have used similar tricks in these kinds of situations.

Make them feel that they're in control too

Narcissists thrive on control as it inflates their egos. So, if you're ever trying to control a narcissist do it by making it seem like they are in control as well, as long as they feel in control they will most likely listen to you. You can do this by giving them various options to choose from, the narcissist will feel like they are the one making the decision while all of them are the options that you prefer. Make sure that the options don't contradict their nature and only pick those that they are more likely to accept.

For example, if you're making a plan with a narcissist, instead of saying "We're going to the movies on Tuesday at 5pm" say, "We're going to the movies on Tuesday, what time are you comfortable with?". This way the narcissist partially feels in control since they helped in making the decision and you get what you want.

Let the narcissist have their way

Sometimes it's just better to let the narcissist be in charge and do what makes them feel better. All narcissist love to take credit for ingenious ideas and solutions, this is a very annoying trait and may even lead to a fight but if it isn't something big, let the narcissist have his way. If you let the narcissist take the credit for something then they will trust you more, they will have a false idea in their head about being in control while you are the one calling the shots.

If you're worried that not taking credit for your own work might be harmful for you then don't let the narcissist take the credit. If the narcissist tries to take the credit don't fight them but explain to them how it's your work.

Controlling Yourself

Don't take things personally

You have to understand that the narcissist does not reflect your behavior. There will be times when you are annoyed by the narcissist, but you have to make sure that you don't take things personally. If you start caring about the narcissist and reciprocating their behavior it will end up badly for you. Remember that all narcissists behave in such a way, they are self-centered and egoistic, it doesn't matter how nice you are to them they cannot show empathy or love.

There are certain limits and boundaries that you need to put in place to they make sure aren't being crossed by the narcissist. If they're latching on to you and trying to bring you down, then it's better to cut off the relationship. Narcissists are very manipulative and will try to hurt you in every way possible. They'll use you to get praise and attention but forget about you as soon as they're exhausted by your company. If you feel that the narcissist is making you feel down then you have to cut them off before it starts harming you. Narcissists love it if people are emotionally unstable because then they are better sources for them to use. They use such people to boost their ego by offering them attention at first, putting them down and then discarding them. This ensures that the person becomes dependent on them.

Don't expect anything from a narcissist

When controlling the narcissist make sure that you do not expect emotional support from them; they'll use you for their own purposes but will never help you out. If you're sad or emotionally unstable the narcissist will look the other way, they just try to benefit from such a situation. It's important that you never ask a narcissist for help or show any weakness in front of them because they are like predators that would use these feelings for their own gain.

This is why narcissists are not good relationship partners; they don't listen to you and only talk about themselves. They are never great sources of emotional support, so make sure that you avoid falling love with narcissists. Most narcissists use a technique where they divide the relationship into three phases and use them to emotionally control you. The first phase starts with being extremely charming and nice to you, you won't even realize that the person is actually a narcissist. They never talk about themselves and only pay attention to you. Many people fall for this sort of behavior since they have never actually experienced a relationship where they were the important one. The second phase is where they try to manipulate you; they will blame you for all that is wrong and make you feel needy. It'll seem like you are unstable and need medical help, while the narcissist is the good one who is trying to help you out. Narcissists do this to make you dependent on them for emotional support, you think that everything is your fault and try to improve yourself to meet their standards. This makes the narcissist feel like a god, as he now has a patron that begs for their attention. The last phase is the discarding phase: the narcissist will leave you without even a second thought and when they leave you will only blame yourself. It can be very difficult to get over such a relationship where you were emotionally controlled and manipulated.

This is why you should never expect the narcissist to be good towards you or help you out in anyway. If you start being more open and develop a very personal bond, the narcissist will just criticize you, everything will be your fault and they'll just make you feel worse.

Take a step back

If you ever feel emotionally exhausted by hanging out with the narcissist you need to be ready to take a step back. Narcissists can be extremely frustrating and difficult to deal with but you have to keep your cool when dealing with such a person. The most important thing is to break off the connection for a while and think about better ways to approach the person. Imagine the situation from an external point of view; a third person perspective is very helpful since it is unbiased and true. You may have been overwhelmed by emotions towards the narcissist or may have taken matters too personally. At this point visualizing the situation from a third party point of view and then thinking about the solution will help you in the long run.

This is also important for your mental health, dealing with a narcissist is not easy and sometimes even talking to them can make you feel overwhelmed. If you feel like you are being emotionally overwhelmed you have to cool down, your mental health is more important than trying to control the narcissist.

Treat them as a human

It is true that narcissists mostly have negative traits that dominate their personality but they are human too and have many positive traits that they just don't show to the world. Don't make the person your enemy, try to approach them using different ways and listen to them. Narcissists can be nice partners or friends if need be, help them by teaching them control.

However, you have to be very subjective and careful of a

narcissist's behavior. They can be nice when they want to be and also very aggressive at times, it all just depends on the circumstances. It is advisable to keep yourself personally and emotionally detached from such people, they are more prone to hurt you than help you.

Control your feelings; do not show negative attitude towards a narcissist. Narcissism is a very unhealthy mental disorder; you have to help a person get over this instead of treating them in a bad manner. Pity them from time to time but do not let it show, if they think that you're showing weakness they will try to take advantage of you.

Chapter 6: Eight Ways to Handle a Narcissist at Work

Believe it to not every single person has a tendency to be a narcissist to some degree or another. Occasionally, you will become involved in a relationship with a person and not realize until somewhere down the line that they are a narcissist – the qualities that first attracted to you now irritate you beyond belief. Or you may have a family member or friend who displays narcissistic traits that you cannot control and find it hard to challenge.

Just because a person is a narcissist, it doesn't make them unlovable. Some people who are narcissist can be good fun, have a lot of charisma and be very good at what they do. Being around them can be pleasurable and they may have a genuinely positive effect on you and those around you. You could, if you chose, try to reform the narcissist in your life rather than walking away and leaving them alone.

Be aware that not all narcissists are the same; it is unfair to tar them all with the same brush and the way you handle the one in your life is entirely down to which type they are. While there are a number of different types, they can be put into two main types –

vulnerable and grandiose:

- **Vulnerable** narcissists have an outward mask of self-absorption and self-centeredness that covers a weak inner person

- **Grandiose** narcissists have a true belief in their own greatness and, in some cases, are actually as good as they believe they are.

Knowing that, take a look at these 8 ways to handle the narcissist in your working life:

1. **Decide Which One.** The vulnerable narcissist will not feel very good about himself or herself deep down. They are not as open with emotion as a grandiose narcissist is and you may not actually realize when they are getting under your feet or undercutting you.

2. **Acknowledge That You Are Annoyed.** Narcissists will easily antagonize you and get in your way so, if you need to get things done and the narcissist is forever interrupting you or putting him or herself in the spotlight, acknowledging the reason for your frustration may be just what you need to stop it once and for all.

3. **Appreciate Where Their Behavior is coming from.** Vulnerable narcissists are forever looking for ways to feel good about themselves, which is why they may start undercutting you. They will probably question your authority but, as soon as you accept that they are insecure, you can give them enough reassurance to settle them into focusing on the task at hand. Be careful – too much reassurance gives them what they want; not enough and you will not have any effect at all.

4. **Evaluate the Context of the Behavior.** Narcissism is not all about one thing – it certainly isn't an all or nothing trait

either. Some situations may make a person more insecure than others and, if the situation doesn't improve, they can turn outright hostile, vindictive and very spiteful.

5. **Be Positive.** If you are working with a narcissist who gets his or her pleasure from seeing someone else suffer, the trick is never to show the pain you feel. That just encourages them more. Don't let them ruffle your feathers, no matter how you feel and their behavior will gradually diminish.

6. **Don't Get Derailed.** When the narcissist takes over it is so easy to lose your sense of purpose or lose sight of your goals. Learn to move ahead without being overly attentive to the narcissist but attentive enough to allay their insecurities.

7. **Maintain Your Humor.** Call a narcissists bluff by ignoring them or by, every now again, joking with them. You don't need to be cruel but you can, in a humorous way, point out how inappropriate their behavior is.

8. **Understand that they need some help.** Some narcissists suffer from a low self-esteem and strong feelings of being inadequate. Because of this, it is vital that you learn to recognize when they may gain benefit from some professional help.

Chapter 7: How To Know If You're In Love With A Narcissist

Everyone wants an ideal relationship where they are heard, and their partner pays attention to them. Ideally, a narcissist is portrayed as someone who only talks about him or herself, but that isn't a true picture. A narcissist is someone who has a definitive picture of themselves in their mind, which is different from reality. Such a person tries to portray him or herself according to this picture, so that their real self is outshined by something in their head. It may get difficult to stay in a relationship with a narcissist but if you proceed with caution, you can help your relationship to get past this small hurdle.

The first step is to make sure that your partner actually suffers from narcissism, some conclusive ways to diagnose your partner are:

Conversation Hoarding

A narcissist loves nothing more than talking about himself/herself. They direct conversations to make sure that they are in the spotlight. It is easy to notice such a behavior if your partner never listens to you and you regularly feel ignored then it may be due to their narcissistic nature. During arguments, if your opinion is mostly dismissed or corrected, then you are definitely in a relationship with a narcissist.

A narcissist loves nothing more than making their opinions seem superior; there are simple ways to control such a behavior. Try to reason with them logically, do not try to overshadow them and never directly contradict them. Slowly and steadily, they will learn to respect your opinions and care about your views as well.

Interrupting Conversations

Have you ever felt like your partner tries to change the topic of the conversations so that it focuses on them? Most people are not comfortable when people talk about them and would never knowingly change the topic of a conversation so that they are in the spotlight. That isn't true for narcissists; they have no hesitation in driving the conversation so that they are the center or attention.

This can be unsettling for most people, because everyone loves to be in the limelight. To ensure that things can like this don't cause problems in your relationship, you should talk to your partner about this and guide them in overcoming this problem.

Breaking Rules

The narcissist loves to break the rules; they like to live dangerously. Even breaking small rules, such as jumping a traffic light or stealing office supplies gives them a thrill. This can be disconcerting for many people; it can make you feel very uncomfortable. There isn't a simple solution to this problem, if you try to reason with them it will be for nothing, you have to understand that a narcissist does not see the world like you. They don't think that it's wrong to break the rules and hence, it is difficult for them to understand why you oppose their actions.

You have to make them understand that they could get in serious trouble if they continue to break rules.

Keep a close eye on them and stop them from doing something rash, even ask their friends to help you with this problem.

Disregard for boundaries

Many narcissists fail to comprehend the invisible boundaries between people and social boundaries that exist in the world. This can make many people uncomfortable as they may not respect your person boundaries and overstep them from time to time. They don't understand the concept of personal space; a relationship can end in days if both the partners don't give each other space from time to time. Sometimes it's important to take a break from your relationship to prevent it from collapsing.

They don't have any regards for boundaries in relation to social situations as well; they may borrow money or items from you and never return them. They may embarrass you in front of a crowd without realizing what they are doing. It's important to make them aware of these boundaries and teach them how they can respect these invisible boundaries.

False Image

Many narcissists try to portray themselves as someone who is perfect and with a lot of achievements. Be it in terms of money or awards, they lie to put a false impression on people. It's very common to hear them gloat about events that make them look good, these events may be cultural, social, academic, and sexual and many others.

It can be exhausting at times to hear them talk about all these false achievements but if you do question them about these things it may offend them. That's because most narcissists try to show themselves as better than other people and when they are questioned about it, it fiddles with their sense of security. Most narcissists cannot bear it if people find out about their true self, instead of the fake self that they portray.

Snobbish behavior

Narcissists can depict snobbish behavior at times. They expect themselves to be entitled and cared for by others. They can think that the world revolves around them and hence expect others to show preferential treatment towards them and cater to their needs without wanting anything in return.

Again, it is not simple to deal with this kind of behavior. It's possible that you might get annoyed because you're not being treated fairly by your partner, but this is a message that you need to give them subtlety. Bring up this topic from time to time and tell them how you have needs to which are not being fulfilled.

Charming Personality

Narcissists are born with charming personalities; they are very impressive and persuasive when they want to be. They use this trait to get things from people, they'll be very considerate for your feelings and needs when they need you but as soon as they get bored or get what they want, they'll drop you. It's important to not fall for someone just because of his or her charm; you have to be careful that they are not using you for their selfish purposes.

Don't hesitate to talk to your partner about this, if you feel like you're being cheated, talk to them about your feeling and try to clear things out without blaming each other.

Superiority Complex

Narcissists suffer from superiority complex; they think that they are more important than other people. They expect to be treated like a prince or a princess while ignoring others needs. They have an aggravated sense of self-importance, and expect to be treated in a grandiose way. They don't ever expect people to leave them; you can even say that they won't ever expect you to break up with them. They think that others can't survive without them and that they are always needed.

It's important that you make these things clear from the starting, do not give them too much important. Care for them, listen to them but never should you make them think that they are the important person in the relationship.

Spreading insecurity

Narcissists live on spreading insecurity and making others look bad. They spread negative emotions, criticize others and ridicule them to make themselves look better. They try to keep their partners off-balance, making comments about your body or emotions that make you feel bad about yourself. This way they try ascertain their importance and boost their ego through others.

Narcissists are also emotionally unstable, so if you try to argue with them or fight them over such things they'll respond by ignoring you or arguing with you. Try to keep yourself stabilized and ensure that these negative comments do not affect you.

Manipulation

Narcissists are very good at manipulating people to serve their own needs. They may emotionally blackmail people close to them, to get things from them such as money or even use them as a ladder to fulfill dreams. Most people don't even notice that they are being manipulated, so it's important to be alert in such relationships to make sure that you're not being used as a pawn.

Chapter 8: Seven Strategies For Dealing With The Narcissist You Love

If you believe that the person you love may be a narcissist but are not sure, take a look at these seven strategies that will give you some clues.

1. **Abuse.** Is your partner either emotionally or physically abusive? Not all narcissists are but some will be and if you are on the receiving end, you should start to look at why you find it hard to walk away. This is your first step. If you are being abused ad you cannot walk away, there is no point in reading any further. If you can find the strength to move on, let's move on.

2. **Denial.** You would know denial if you saw it; it is the number one of all defense mechanisms. The more denial your narcissist exhibits, the less chance there is of being able to help them change. Can your partner admit when they are wrong or when something is wrong about their life? Some narcissists do recognize what they are going through and will seek help, usually a vulnerable narcissist, and they are more likely to stay with a treatment plan once it's underway.

3. **Manipulation.** Manipulative narcissists can be very aggressive, and can exhibit desires to cheat, steal, or even damage property. Entitlement and exploitation are the worst behaviors that a narcissist can display and individuals who present with these symptoms may even be closer to being a psychopath. Not all narcissists will be cold and calculating but those that are will pose the biggest threat, will struggle to separate fiction from fact and are practiced at deceiving people.

4. **Willingness to Change.** It might seem an obvious one but it is also a vital one. Test your partner's willingness to change by suggesting that you seek help from a couple's therapist. Not everyone likes the thought of therapy so don't consider this to be the test that lights the fire. If your partner agrees to the therapy, it does show that there is hope for the relationship.

5. **Anger.** Your partner will hurl insults at you; will tell you that you've always been paranoid and jealous when you question the amount of time he or she spends with another person of the opposite sex. Of course, when you get told things like that, your natural instinct is to protect yourself and for many, that involves a full-scale battle, an attack on your partner with you accusing them of being the selfish one. It's natural but is it the right reaction? Unfortunately, anger stops of from receiving vital information, it stops you from knowing if your partner can see the fear and the sadness you may feel at losing them and if it moves them at all. Where possible, anger should be kept in check and feelings shared on a vulnerable level that all parties can respond to.

6. **Silence.** Let's assume that you've got home after a really hard day and your partner stars moaning about your plans for the weekend not being settled. He or she will moan that you can't make decisions and that you are totally indecisive about anything. Condescension doesn't always provoke anger. If your self-esteem is already low, those kinds of remarks just serve to

shut you down and bring on the silence. But, if you want things to improve you have to speak up. Withdrawal into silence is a way of coping but it isn't always the right way. The silent treatment can serve to make a narcissist feel even more insecure and that manifests itself in several ways, usually more criticism or total indifference to you and your feelings.

7. **Honesty.** If you've tried the loving and soft approach to telling your partner the things the hurt about your relationship and your narcissistic partner still won't give in, you really have done everything that you can. Staying in a relationship that is unhappy will cost you dearly so you need to be honest with yourself and ask why you are staying with this person.

Arrogance and hostility is not good at the best of times but when it comes from a narcissist, it can be truly gut wrenching. It can also serve to get right under your skin. A natural response in the face of this kind of behavior is to pull back or lash out but sharing your feelings openly and honestly with your partner may be the only chance they get at actually hearing what you are saying and feeling. If they don't respond and don't understand the pain you are feeling at that point then, in all likelihood, they probably never will. As hard and hurtful as it may be, if this is the situation you are in, the best thing you can do to save yourself is to walk away.

Chapter 9: How Narcissists Try To Get Inside Your Head

Narcissist is a word commonly used these days and applies to people who are self-absorbed or vain. Narcissism in essence is about being self-absorbed but as a serious psychological disorder it is very different. Narcissists can be very dangerous; they are extremely anti-social and also manipulative. If you're in a relationship with a narcissist it's possible that they try to get into your head to assert their dominance over you. They make you feel less important and shallow, so that their own qualities outshine yours.

It's important in any relationship to set boundaries, make sure that this manipulation isn't affecting your health and well-being. There are simple ways to identify if you're being used by a narcissist for his or her own pleasure.

Relationship Games

Relationships with Narcissists usually have three phases, at all of these phases they try to manipulate in you in some way or the other. Now, this manipulation is almost always for personal gain. The first phase is known as Idealization, the phase where they give you the most importance. This phase is usually in the first months of dating/being in a relationship, Narcissists are born charmers and they always make you feel like you're the most important person in the field. They constantly message you, lost to whatever you're saying and make you feel like the center of attention. This all is pretense so that they can build a strong trust inside you for them, which they can use for their own advantage at a later period. This is all to convince you that you have finally found your soul mate whom you can't live without, most of the people never find someone who takes care of them and only cares about them so many of them blindly trust narcissists when they offer comfort and care. Most people are tired of the games that people play in relationships and the constant lying, so it's easy to fall for a guy who puts you on a pedestal. You need to be wary of constant texting, unnecessary compliments and unwavering attention. The motive is to make it seem like they're actually interested in you but all they want is for you to be dependent on their opinions and attention.

The second phase is known as devaluation. This is the phase where the narcissist unfolds his cards. Now, that they have you hooked to their attention and care, they'll try control your feelings by making it seem that everything wrong with your relationship if your fault. You'll suddenly feel like you have in all those previous relationships, you won't be the center of attention anymore and they will try to control you by comparing you to others, arguing with you and making you feel insecure. They'll make it seem like it's entirely yours fault and slowly withdraw from you, give you the silent treatment and put you down. Finally, you'll be convinced that you created all the problems and have led to the end of the relationship.

The narcissists are actually the jealous ones who need constant attention and praise; narcissists try to project these feelings on you. Since you are accustomed to their constant attention, their withdrawal might hit you hard and would make you crave for their presence again. In this way you become the clingy one who needs him/her all the time. The only solution left with you would be to not be the needy one so that your partner will love you the same way he did in the beginning of the relationship. All of this is to control your emotions, make you feel inconsiderate about your feelings so that the narcissist himself can pave a way for his huge ego.

It is very difficult to cope with such a behavior, but you have to understand that the man in the beginning of the relationship didn't exist at all, they presented you with a false image and now that they show their true colors it's difficult to imagine the relationship you dreamed of in the starting.

The last phase is discarding. The narcissist leaves a person in such a way that they are left emotionally unstable. The methods are always similar; it's violence, public humiliation or aggressive behavior. It leaves a person thinking that they are worthless and can never have a good life.

Manipulation

In a relationship with a narcissist it will always be your fault, every problem is due to your behavior and needs. Most narcissists use the technique of gas lighting to manipulate you so that you believe that sowed the seeds of discord in the relationship. It starts with shallow comments about your instability, how you have psychological problems that need to be checked out and the narcissist may even force you to consult a specialist. Such things should not be taken lightly because they are categorized as mental abuse and if you find out that you're being manipulated it's time to take some serious steps.

It'll always be the narcissist who depicts aggressive behavior and violent outbursts but they'll try to make you believe that you were the one provoking them and it's you issues that cause them to be violent. It's all a game of falsehood and insecurity; they are like leeches that feed on your discomfort because it boasts their ego.

In the end, you are left with nothing but doubts and misinterpretations. You will feel like you could have stopped the relationship from breaking up by controlling your needs, which is absolutely false and is an idea that has been invested inside you by the narcissist.

Doubts and Discord

Narcissists don't think twice before putting people down harshly. Expect to be told that harsh truths that make you feel bad about yourself; these may be true or may be not but will always make you feel insufficient. The narcissist only wants to portray himself as the important one and you as just someone who makes mistakes and causes problems. They need you to admire them so that their own image of self-importance increases every day. The perfect way for this is to make you doubt yourself and look towards them for attention. Beware of their friends as well, it won't be a surprise if they have the same personality disorder as your partner and are just helping him/her achieve their goals by emotionally manipulating you.

After the discard phase, they'll try to start a smear campaign against you, spread rumors and paint you as the clingy and unstable one who drove them away. What they accomplish from all of this are three important things:

- It shows you as the one who is unstable; you provoked them to act so abusive and aggressive. It'll all be your fault, even in the eyes of your own friends. You will loathe yourself and won't even recollect the things you said, you will just believe what you are told,

- It's not like you won't be provoked either, you'll also lash out and act aggressive. This will just be like adding fuel to the fire; the lie that they created about you being unstable would slowly turn into truth.
- The final accomplishment would be that you'd still get back in the relationship even after being abused and controlled. The only way to deal with this is to completely seclude yourself from the narcissist and anyone else who tries to bring you down or blames you for all the mistakes.

Inviting Third Parties

The narcissist tries to make you feel worse by inviting other people to your relationship. This method of emotional control is known as triangulation, the narcissist uses your insecurity to make it seem like there are better people for them than you. This can be anyone an ex-lover, a current affair, a neighbor or friend. This way they make you compete for their love and there is nothing that a narcissist loves more than people fighting for their attention.

You were already the less important one in the relationship but now you're being forced to sacrifice even more to keep the relationship going. The narcissist sows this seed of jealousy inside you and makes you feel worse about yourself. It'll start with small things such as making it obvious that they are having an affair or having intense arguments with you about your future. In a regular relationship such things would have been dealt calmly by taking it out but the narcissist doesn't think twice about flirting or having an affair, they'll go right ahead as long as it makes you feel insecure. You're just so busy looking at ways to compete with this other person that you forget about the abuse that you are facing and how it's demeaning you day by day.

The two images of the Narcissist

It's very difficult to identify a narcissist. They are born charmers and wouldn't make you ever doubt that they are manipulating you.

There are two images of the narcissist, one that he portrays to the world and the actual one. The image that a narcissist portrays is actually a fictional one that they have in their head, they act and talk like this person to make it seem that they are better than their true self. So, you'll never really know that this sweet and charming person you're talking to might be trying to create instability in your life. The true self of a narcissist is a jealous and very insecure image, the only way that they are able to maintain the other image is by feeding off attention and praise that they get from others. This is why the narcissist tries to act like the more important one in a relationship, so that you boast their ego by craving for their attention. Even after the narcissist shows his true colors in the discard phase it can still be difficult to imagine this abusive person as the same person who loved you all those months ago. Which is why it is difficult for many people to let go of the narcissist even after they depict their aggressive behavior, they just pass it off as a bad phase and expect things to back to the first days of the relationship when they were the center of attention. The doubts have sowed so deep in your mind that you even try to improve yourself to meet the narcissist's standards; you blame yourself for proving them and bringing out their aggressive behavior. It can be a long time before you start believing in yourself and realize that none of this was your fault.

The only time you can definitely diagnose someone with a narcissistic personality disorder us during the discard phase. It is during this phase that you see the real face of the narcissist that they had been hiding behind the sweetness and charm. You realize that they never had any love for you and that you were nothing more than an instrument to feed their ego. The silent treatment, the blaming and aggressive behavior are all signs that you need to end the relationship before you're too emotionally unstable to return to your former self.

It's finally time to realize what you were to them, a source of supply to feed their ego and nothing more. The love and attention that you were given at the starting of the relationship is no more, the charming and sweet person has now finally shown their true colors. Narcissists do not feel any love for you after they have discarded you, it was all a façade and now their goal has been achieved so it's time to break all ties. This is what you should do as well, forget about all the negativity that you received because of them and move on. Remember that the connection you felt in the starting has ended and the person you lived was a sociopath who never really cared about you.

Chapter 10: Walking Away From A Narcissist

So, you've made the decision, you are going to walk away and leave your narcissistic partner behind for good. Perhaps, before you do so, you should understand a few things about narcissists that may make it easier for you to walk away. Once you get a handle on what to expect, you can come up with a plan for dealing with it. So, here goes:

- **Narcissists Do Not Like Losing**

They really don't. When you say that your relationship is finished, you mean it but the narcissist you are talking to sees that as you throwing down a gauntlet, an invitation to kick into high narcissistic mode and see it as a real challenge and that leads you to:

- **Narcissists Pursue Victory**

He or she won't be chasing after you although that's what it will look like. No, instead they are looking to put things back to how they should be, with them in full control and you bowing down and taking the abuse, while smothering them in adoration and praise. Believe me when I say this, if you give in and do go back, there will be some form of punishment for the abandonment. He or she does want you back but only on their terms and with the same, if not a higher, degree of selfishness and narcissistic behavior that was there when you left – why you left.

- **Narcissists Want to Keep a Constant Check on You**

Because he or she still loves you? Not likely. Let's face it; they probably never really loved you in the true sense. All he or she wants to do is make sure that you are suffering, that you are not happy and never will be without them in your life. To a narcissist, it is the knowledge that you are truly miserable and suffering without him or her is as satisfying as getting you to go back to them.

At the end of the day, if he or she cannot keep your attention on him or her throughout the relationship then they will want to know that you are constantly thinking of them and really struggling after you are apart. At some point, he or she will offer to end the suffering by accepting your apology and taking you back. Big mistake – once you are back under their control the abuse will begin again and it will never stop. The most satisfying thing to a narcissist is having you swaying between being with him or her and leaving – that gives the control over you, the ultimate prize for a narcissist.

- **Go Cold Turkey**

This is seriously the only way you can break free of a narcissistic relationship. There is no way that you can still be friends because that means he or she still has a degree of control over you. Dumped narcissists are not going to be normal ex-partners; you cannot share the odd text or email with them. Any contact leaves you open to abuse and hurt and he or she will find that chink in your armor. Every text message, email, phone call, even a chance encounter will set you back and will extend your recovery time. There is no way for you to heal if you are still suffering so you must stay completely away, no contact whatsoever.

In terms of ex-partners, there are a couple of different types that you should know about:

- **The Herpes Narcissist**

This is the type of narcissist who never goes away, will always reappear when you least expect it. He or she will appear and expect to pick up where they left off, as if nothing happened, as if you were just having a bit of a tiff – he'll forgive you and it's all fine now. He or she will act like this even if you have had no contact for several months, even if you have had to take the step of getting a restraining order. In his or her eyes this is devotion and love, but believe me, it is not. If, in one weak moment, you warm up to him or her, you will be sucked back in, he or she will take delight in reminding you why you left in the first place and you will be back to square one.

- **The Lyme Disease Narcissist**

This one will go away but not until you have been fighting and defending yourself for months on end. This will leave you broken, exhausted, and scarred with reminders of what you have been through. If you were unlucky enough to have been married and have children with the narcissist, your divorce is going to be turned into a living hell, in much the same way as your marriage was. He or she will give the impression that they simply can't wait to get away from you and will them proceed to impede the divorce and stall as much as he or she possible can. This is just their way of showing you who is in full control. And that is before the true nightmare will start – custody arrangements. You must be strong to get through this and you must realize that, until the children are grown up, you will still have to have some contact with him or her.

- **The Itchy Rash Narcissist**

This is the best one really. You know that there is only one way to deal with an itchy rash – ignore it. It doesn't matter how annoying it is, it doesn't matter that you know attending to it will give you the relief you need, ignoring it is the only way to make it go away. And it's the same for the narcissist. Ignore them for long enough and they will go away of their own accord – eventually.

- **The Train Wreck Narcissist**

On very rare occasions, you will be dealing with a train wreck narcissist. These will, very suddenly and without any warning at all, leave. They may get a hint of your intentions to go and they will probably cool off on the abuse for a bit. But, all of a sudden, they will inflict cruel, harsh abuse on you and then leave – they perceive it as abandoning you before you can do it to them. The result will not be attractive, they will leave you deeply devastated and hurt, not because they have gone but because of the manner they did it in. But, this is often the best outcome; you will never have to deal with them again because they will never appear near you or try to make contact with you. In their eyes, they are still in control because they left the relationship; they dumped you. This allows you to recover without any interference.

Chapter 11: Why Is It So Difficult to Stay Away From A Narcissist?

There are many people who have never been in a relationship with a narcissist and do not understand why it is so difficult to stay away from one. Even when we know what they are capable of, how toxic they are, we still cannot stay away. Putting aside the qualities that drew us to them in the first place, like the obvious charm, the most important thing to remember is how a narcissist works – by brainwashing. Its how they make us keep on going back for more, how they hook us. Understanding exactly how they do this is the key to your recovery.

The narcissist is a master manipulator. They know exactly how to make us feel guilty for things we haven't done or said enough to make us go crawling back, begging for forgiveness. They know exactly how to make us want to offer to help them, to feel so sorry for them that we will lay down our lives at their feet. And they know exactly how to make promises that things will be so different this time around that we feel we should go back to them and give them another chance. The last thing they know how to do is make us doubt ourselves. At the end of the day, they have us trained, trained to return at the click of a finger to go back to them over and over, similar to the way we train a dog to return to us when we call them.

In the study of behaviorism, there is a principle called Random Reinforcement. This explains how responses to identical behavior can be inconsistent, which leads to addiction. It's the same principle as gambling and pushing money into a slot machine – you get a huge reward when you do something on one occasion, but on other occasions that same method results in a huge loss or a punishment of some kind.

There is always the thrill, the thought that the next time you will get the reward again and we keep on chasing the high we got from when we did win. Think of being with a narcissist is like being on a rollercoaster ride, one with some incredible highs and some totally unbelievable and devastating lows. One minute it is exciting, the next scarily demoralizing and demeaning.

We hope that if we keep on chasing that high, we can get through the worst of the lows and we will see that reward once again – and you will, but only fleetingly. The good times ever come back on a permanent basis and by giving us rewards on an intermittent basis the narcissist keeps us hooked. They are the best manipulators in the world and they know exactly what they are doing. It's safe to say that a narcissist enjoys doling out the punishment as much, if not more than giving rewards.

When you are in a long-term relationship with a narcissist, you've been together for years; you start to doubt your own abilities to make any decisions. At the end of the day, for as long as you have been together, the narcissist has controlled everything, every move we make. They spend the time training us and conditioning us to go to them for answers and that takes away our ability to think for ourselves. We end up terrified that we are going to be left alone and we have no trust in our instincts anymore. A narcissist will also keep us isolated, away from friends and family so we no longer have a support system.

Let's just digress for one moment. Have you ever heard of something called the Stockholm Syndrome? It is a psychological phenomenon, a situation in which a hostage will bond with his or her captors. The name comes from a robbery at the Kreditbanken in Norrmalmstorg, Stockholm when bank robbers held a number of employees hostage for 5 days, between august 23 and 28 in 1793. The victims, the hostages bonded emotionally with their captors and, after their release, they could be heard defending the robbers. Nils Bejerot, a psychiatrist and criminologist who helped the police in the case, produced the term, Stockholm syndrome.

There is a lot of debate over the factors that may or may not contribute to the syndrome but, at the end of the day, every abuser has the same goal – control, ensuring that the victim is totally reliant and dependent on him or her for their survival. Key components of the syndrome are continuous contact, a long period of time before resolution and emotional against physical abuse. These are the same components that come into play in a long-term relationship with a narcissist and this goes a long way towards explaining why it is so difficult to walk away and to stay away.

This is also often known as trauma bonding, simply because the narcissist has us so conditioned into believing that we can't survive without them that we can't walk away. It is their way of confusing us and keeping us in that emotional state, a way of making us turn and walk back to them, no matter what the consequences. And it is for this reason that the only way to break free from a narcissist is to invoke the No Contact rule.

The only people that can help us to recover are others who have been through the exact same thing. They are the only ones who can support us and help us to deprogram ourselves and to stop us from having any contact with the narcissist.

Anyone who is going through this right now – celebrate it, celebrate every single minute, hour, day, week and month that you have no contain with the ex-narcissist in your life because each one of those is another step towards freedom. Never punish yourself if you fail – recovery takes time and it's all about progress, never about perfection. If you go off course, forget about it. Just get back on track and continue on your way. Do give yourself time to consider why you went off course first so that you know not to make the same mistake again.

"Progress means getting nearer to the place you want to be. And if you have taken a wrong turning, then to go forward does not get you any nearer. If you are on the wrong road, progress means doing an about-turn and walking back to the right road; and in that case the man who turns back soonest is the most progressive man."
– C.S. Lewis

Conclusion

Narcissists can be the nicest people on earth at first look, and some will remain as charming as the day you first met them. Others will turn as soon as they have hooked you. Either way, a relationship with a narcissist is going to be a bumpy ride. For many, it's a ride they never manage to get off of, a ride that they will go through life experiencing and for others it's a ride that they do manage to escape from but not without some cost to themselves.

Life with a narcissist is emotionally draining, and physically. It can leave you scarred for life and scared to approach another relationship. But, by withdrawing into your shell and not living the life you deserve to have, you are giving the narcissist exactly what he or she wants – control of your life, a control they will never let go of until you cut the cord.

I hope that my book has been of some help to you and you now have a better understanding of narcissists and how they operate. If you did find this book helpful, please be so kind as to leave a review to help me provide you with more beneficial books and resources!

You May Enjoy James Seal's Other Books

Personality Disorders: Borderline Personality Disorder: Beauty Queen or Emotional Terrorist?

hyperurl.co/emotionalterror

NLP Subconscious Mind Power: Change Your Mind Change Your Life

hyperurl.co/NLP

Creativity : Creative Thinking To Improve Memory, Increase Success and Live A Healthy Life

hyperurl.co/creative

SELF ESTEEM: Confidence Building: Overcome Fear, Stress and Anxiety: Self Help Guide

hyperurl.co/selfesteem

Personality Disorders: NARCISSISM: How To Survive A Narcissistic Relationship

hyperurl.co/narcissism

Psychopath: Inside The Mind Of Predators and Con Men: Personality Disorders

hyperurl.co/psychopath

Anger: Natural Treatments To Manage Frustration And Stress

hyperurl.co/anger